The Bible and Christian Living

DAVID FIELD

The Bible can be read as great literature, or as a history of Israel, or as a source-book of theological information. It is all of these things. But none of them does full justice to the purpose of Scripture as set out by the Bible writers themselves, or to the cumulative experience of Bible users through the centuries.

When Ezra the scribe read from the law of Moses to the returned exiles in Jerusalem, the people, we are told, not only 'understood the reading' but alternately 'wept when they heard the words of the law' and made 'great rejoicing'. And they came back the next day to build shelters for the Feast of Tabernacles, in obedience to the law's commands. The act of hearing and understanding the scriptures had aroused their emotions and stirred them to action.

Nehemiah 8

Centuries after Ezra, J. B. Phillips describes his similar experience in translating the New Testament. 'Although I did my utmost to preserve an emotional detachment,' he writes, 'I found again and again that the material under my hands was strangely alive; it spoke to my condition in the most uncanny way.'

These reactions accurately reflect the vivid metaphors we find in the Bible, used by its writers to describe the impact God's word made in their own experience. It is a fire to warm and a hammer to break, water to cleanse, milk to nourish, meat to invigorate, light to guide, a sword for the fight, and a mirror to reveal. It is 'at work in you believers', 'able to build you up', 'living and active…piercing…discerning'.

Jeremiah 23:29; 1 Peter 2:2;
Hebrews 5:13-14; Psalm 119:105;
Ephesians 6:17; James 1:23-25;
1 Thessalonians 2:13; Acts 20:32;
Hebrews 4:12

THE BIBLE IS RELEVANT

All this means that the reader who approaches the Bible in a purely detached way is in danger of failing to appreciate its primary purpose, which is a practical, dynamic one. Its aim is to *do something* in the life of the person who reads it, as well as to capture his aesthetic interest and supply him with historical and theological information. The huge cultural gaps which separate Bible times from our own make such a purpose all the more remarkable, but the Bible can justify its claim to contemporary relevance in two ways.

In the first place, it deals with those elements in *human nature* which are timeless. The men and women we read about in the Bible have aspirations and failings with which we easily identify, and even the heroes of Scripture are displayed in the cold light of truth. As Augustine put it, 'The sacred record, like a faithful mirror, has no flattery in its portraits.'

Then, secondly, the truths of the Bible are ever-relevant because *God himself* does not change, either in his nature or in his dealings with men. Through reading the Bible we discover fundamental truths about God, and see them demonstrated by events in the lives of his people which illuminate his character and illustrate his will for all men at all times. So it is that even events from the distant past 'were written down for *our* instruction' in order that in the present and for the future 'by the encouragement of the scriptures we might have hope'.

1 Corinthians 10:11; Romans 15:4

THE BIBLE IS PRACTICAL

The Bible, then, retains its contemporary bite. What are the practical purposes it aims to achieve?

It points people to Jesus

The purpose of John's Gospel is clearly set out: 'Now Jesus did many other signs in the presence of the disciples, which are not written in this book; but these are written that you may believe that Jesus is the Christ, the Son of God, and that believing you may have life in his name.'

John 20:30-31

In writing with this frankly propagandist aim – to focus on Jesus Christ – the disciple was being faithful to the remarkable way in which his Master summed up the purpose of *all* Scripture. 'You search the scriptures', Jesus once replied to his critics, 'because you think that in them you have eternal life; and it is they that bear witness to *me*. If you believed Moses, you would believe me, for he wrote of *me*.'

John 5:39, 46

Not surprisingly, the listening disciples were slow to grasp the full meaning of these words. After the resurrection Jesus had to rebuke them for their dull-ness before showing them once again – and this time more explicitly – how, like the spokes of a wheel, the whole message of the Bible converged on himself. 'Beginning with Moses and all the prophets, he inter-preted to them in all the scriptures the things concern-

Luke 24:27

THE LION
Bible User's
Starter Kit

A LION BOOK

Introducing The Lion Bible User's Starter Kit

Contents

For millions of people down the ages the Bible has been, and still is, a book to live by. Its words are extraordinarily alive and powerful. It speaks to people today. And to understand it the first requirement is to *want* to get to grips with it, to hear what God may have to say to us through its pages. But it also helps if we can find out something of the background to each book: time and place, writer and readers or hearers. For the Bible is of course an amazing collection of ancient documents. That is where this little book comes in.

All the material between these covers comes from *The Lion Handbook to the Bible*. It includes some of the charts and maps. And what this Starter Kit does for Mark's Gospel the *Handbook* does for the whole Bible. So we hope you will find this an 'appetizer', as well as a useful pocket guide in its own right. The first article shows the relevance of the Bible today. The chart shows, step-by-step, how we can understand the Bible. More charts give a birds-eye view of the historical background to the Old and New Testaments. Maps make it easy to see where particular events actually took place.

Faced with a big book (in fact a whole library of books!) such as the Bible, it is hard to know where to begin. Mark's Gospel, the shortest and most action-packed of the four accounts of Jesus' life is a good starting-point. The *Handbook* was written to encourage readers to look at the Bible books as a whole. It is important – and an exhilarating experience – for anyone coming new to the Bible to get an overview, before tackling the detail. Where better to begin than with the life of Jesus – with mini-maps, photographs and a basic guide giving notes on difficult points, to help.

It works with any version of the Bible, so just open the one on your bookshelf, or get a good modern translation, and start reading! We hope you will enjoy this first taste so much that you will soon be back for more.

ing himself'. And Luke goes on to tell us that Jesus drew special attention to those passages from the Old Testament which spoke of his death and resurrection, as a stimulus to repentance and the basis for forgiveness of sins.

Jesus clearly believed that the main aim of the (Old Testament) scriptures was to point people to himself; which meant in practice (if we add Luke's evidence to John's), that through repentance and faith men and women should find the forgiveness and life which he had died and risen to make possible for them.

By their preaching and writing, the apostles showed that they had finally grasped Jesus' point that the Bible's main practical purpose is to draw people to himself as their Saviour. 'To him', preached Peter, 'all the prophets bear witness, that every one who believes in him receives forgiveness of sins through his name.' James pleaded with his readers to 'receive with meekness the implanted word, which is able to save your souls'. Paul reminded Timothy 'how from childhood you have been acquainted with the sacred writings which are able to instruct you for salvation through faith in Christ Jesus'.

Acts 10:43

James 1:21

2 Timothy 3:15

It builds a relationship with God

In Martin Luther's words, just as a mother goes to the cradle only to find the baby, we go to the Bible only to find Christ. It is the Bible's primary purpose to bring men to their Saviour by arousing the beginnings of faith. But this is not the only practical function it aims to fulfil. Peter and the author of the letter to the Hebrews use the analogy of birth and growth to illustrate a further purpose of Scripture. Those who have put their trust in Jesus as Saviour 'have been born anew . . . through the living and abiding word of God'; but, like all new-born babes, they must 'long for the pure spiritual milk' of the word if they are to survive and grow; and once beyond babyhood they need solid food – which is the 'meat' of God's word.

1 Peter 1:23

1 Peter 2:2

Hebrews 5:12-14

This growth process is, above all, a growing up in relationship with God. It is the Bible's function to feed the personal knowledge of the Father which the Christian 'child' enjoys. And 'enjoy' is exactly the right word, because as the believer learns more about God his delight becomes more intense. That is why Bible study should never be dull for a Christian. 'Your words', cries out Jeremiah, 'became to me a joy and the delight of my heart; for I am called by your name, O Lord, God of hosts.' Any personal relationship is fostered by words, and through the pages of his Bible the Christian

Jeremiah 15:16

hears God speaking to him; an experience, says the Psalmist, that is 'sweeter than honey'.

Psalm 19:10

If this sounds like love-letter language we should not be surprised, because the relationship into which God invites believers is a love-relationship. His, however, is a love which makes exacting demands. The information about God and his will which the Christian receives through reading the Bible calls for a tough response that is anything but sentimental. 'If a man loves me', Jesus taught, 'he will *keep* my word, and my Father will love him, and we will come to him and make our home with him…and the word which you hear is not mine but the Father's who sent me.'

John 14:23-24

It equips for battle

Such a stern demand is appropriate because once a man becomes a Christian he finds himself enlisted on God's side in a lifelong battle. He is called upon both to defend his faith against stiff opposition and to spread it among his friends. For both operations, offensive and defensive, his chief weapon is the Bible. It is the 'sword of the Spirit', declares Paul, with which he can combat hostile ideas and cut a straight path for God's truth into the innermost strongholds of the human will.

Ephesians 6:17

Hebrews 4:12

Jesus himself set the pattern for this very practical use of the Bible in his own ministry. Honest enquirers, like the lawyer who asked him about the greatest commandment, were impressed and attracted by his Bible-based teaching (though, as with the rich young ruler, they did not all respond to it positively). On the other hand Jesus fought off false teaching, whether the arguments of men like the Sadducees or the insidious suggestions of the arch-enemy in the desert, with the words of his Bible. Bible words do not have magical powers in themselves, but because all words express ideas, and ideas lie behind action, the word of God is a mighty weapon to influence men's convictions and conduct. Jesus fought his battles with his own words and with the words of his Bible, and he sent his disciples out to preach both.

Mark 12:28-34

Matthew 19:16-22

Matthew 22:23-33

Matthew 4:1-11

This gives the Christian all the incentive he needs to fill his mind with Bible doctrine. Without (for example) a grasp of what the Bible teaches about human nature he will soon be speechless before the claims of twentieth-century humanism. If he is vague about the meaning of Christ's death and resurrection, he cannot hope to introduce others to Jesus as their Saviour. Hence the insistence of the later books of the New Testament that anyone who aims to serve Christ faithfully must make it his aim to know and conserve God's truth. 'Guard the truth that has been entrusted to you by the Holy Spirit', writes Paul to Timothy, 'and what you have heard from me before many witnesses entrust to faithful men who will be able to teach others also.'

2 Timothy 1:14; 2:2

It guides conduct

In his earlier letter to Timothy, Paul had already drawn attention to the importance of maintaining right standards of conduct alongside right beliefs. To 'wage the good warfare' involves 'holding faith *and a good conscience*.' The one cannot be made a substitute for the other; indeed, any failure in right conduct inevitably brings about a downfall in right beliefs. 'By rejecting conscience, certain persons have made shipwreck of their faith'. This is a major Bible theme. In the Old Testament, farmer Amos, with rustic bluntness, flays those who attempt to keep up a religious façade without matching conduct; and James, his outspoken New Testament counterpart, exposes those who are 'hearers of the word' but not 'doers' of it. Jesus makes the same point in his parable of the two builders.

1 Timothy 1:18-19

James 1:22

Matthew 7:24-27

The same pressures which threaten to muddle his faith can seduce the Christian into moral laxity; but the Bible, which provides his main line of defence

2 Timothy 3:16

Philippians 2:13

See Romans 14

Hebrews 13:21

against false teaching, is also an effective weapon against moral temptations. It sets out, by example as well as by direct command, the differences between right and wrong, so that the man who measures his conduct by Bible standards gains from it both 'reproof' when he is in the wrong and 'correction' to set him back on a right course. The Bible becomes his bastion against moral powerlessness, too, by reminding him constantly of the divine power that is available to overcome his weakness ('for God is at work in you, both to *will* and to *work* for his good pleasure'). The man who knows and claims the Bible's promises is empowered to live a kind of life which would otherwise be completely beyond his grasp.

The moral commands of the Bible are presented more as main guiding principles and ideals than as a set of meticulously detailed regulations for daily living. They reach behind right actions to right motives, and their application may differ from person to person according to circumstances. Goodness is defined as that which pleases God, so the Christian with a clear conscience is the one who is totally absorbed with pleasing him. And, as we have already seen, it is the Bible's function to feed and foster such a relationship.

THE BIBLE IS FOR ORDINARY PEOPLE

The Bible is not written in a secret spiritual code which must be cracked if its message is to be understood. Provided it is read sensibly (see the section 'Understanding the Bible'), it is clear enough for the simplest Christian to live by, as well as being profound enough to exercise the mind of the brightest scholar for a lifetime. The decisive qualifications for profitable Bible study are spiritual rather than intellectual.

Among the qualities which the Bible itself suggests, the following are particularly prominent:

Families and groups in homes and churches throughout the world gather with one simple aim: to discover what the Bible says and apply it to their own situation today. The Bible is not just a book of the past. It is read by more people today than ever before.

A will to obey

John 7:17

'Whoever has the will to do the will of God', said Jesus, 'shall know whether my teaching comes from him.' This is a fundamental requirement, if the teaching of the Bible is going to make its full impact on any reader's life. It has been well said that 'the Bible is never mastered by the reader who refuses its mastery of him'.

Concentration

Words calling for sustained effort ('search', 'meditate', 'examine') are used in the Bible to describe the way the scriptures must be read for maximum benefit. *'Concentrate* on winning God's approval, on being a *workman* with nothing to be ashamed of, and who knows how to

2 Timothy 2:15, Phillips

use the word of truth to the best advantage.'

Patience

Hebrews 6:12

It is 'through faith and patience' that the Bible's promises are to be obtained. Patient conviction that God's word is to be trusted will bring the believer

See Hebrews 11.17-19

through times of perplexity.

Persistence

Luke 8:18

Jesus' promise and warning, 'To him who has will more be given, and from him who has not, even what he thinks that he has will be taken away', was made in the context of hearing the word of God. To the persistent seeker the Bible yields more and more of its riches.

Submission to the Holy Spirit

Luke 24:45

When Jesus met his disciples after the resurrection 'he opened their minds to understand the scriptures', by relating what they read in their Bibles to what was happening around them. It is through the prompting of the Holy Spirit that the Bible reader gains the mind of Christ, which enables him to apply teaching given centuries ago to contemporary life.

See 1 Corinthians 2:9-16

It would be impossible to better Paul's summary of the practical and devotional potential of the Bible: 'Your mind has been familiar with the holy scriptures, which can open the mind to the salvation which comes through believing on Christ Jesus. All scripture is inspired by God and is useful for teaching the faith and correcting error, for re-setting the direction of a man's life and training him in good living. The scriptures are the comprehensive equipment of the man of God, and

2 Timothy 3:15-17, Phillips

fit him fully for all branches of his work.'

The Bible was written centuries ago to people in a very different culture from our own.

These stages in understanding and applying it will help avoid:

- picking a bit out of context. The Bible is *not* a magic box!
- building a doctrine on a verse which has been misunderstood — as frequently done by cults and deviations.
- saying it's too remote and difficult for ordinary people: it's not!
- reading it just as literature or geography or history: it *is* these things, but *more*: it's the message that matters.
- reading it as magic, or fables, or fairy-stories ... the Bible was written by real people in real situations as they were inspired by God.

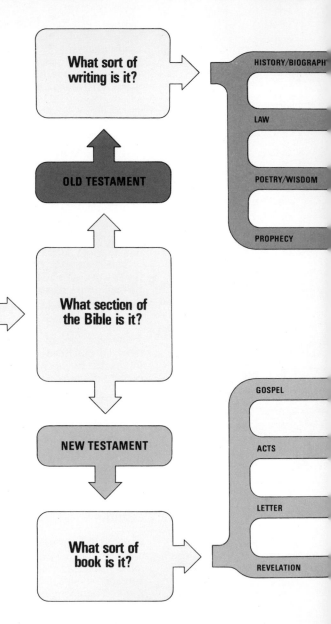

What sort of writing is it?

HISTORY/BIOGRAPHY

LAW

POETRY/WISDOM

PROPHECY

OLD TESTAMENT

What section of the Bible is it?

NEW TESTAMENT

GOSPEL

ACTS

LETTER

REVELATION

What sort of book is it?

What happened? Where? To whom? Why was the story told? Is this a story-with-a-point?

Is this moral law, for all time? Or matters of social or ceremonial law? If the latter, what point was being expressed, or general principle?

Don't read poetry as if it's prose! Expect imagery, picture language. Instead of rhyme, Hebrew poetry said things twice in different words.

What was the historical setting, the story behind the passage? Is the writing poetic, symbolic? What was the original purpose of the prophecy?

What did the passage mean to the original readers or hearers? How does the same message apply today?

Four accounts of the teaching and events of the life of Jesus. Is the passage narrative or a story-with-a-point (parable)?

What happened? Was the story included to make a special point?

Who was writing to whom — and why? (See e.g. beginning of letter) What is the main point or argument of the letter as a whole? How does the passage fit into this?

Set against Roman persecution, John used 'apocalyptic' literary style: Old Testament and poetic imagery. Read with imagination, emotion to get the universal point.

● Does it add to our understanding of a particular doctrine?

● Does it give us a better understanding of God, Jesus, the Holy Spirit, leading to praise and prayer?

● How does it apply in our own lives, or in our church or local community?

The Bible still speaks with remarkable clarity to our own time. With much of the Bible there is no problem in understanding it: simply read it!

OLD TESTAMENT HISTORY AT A GLANCE

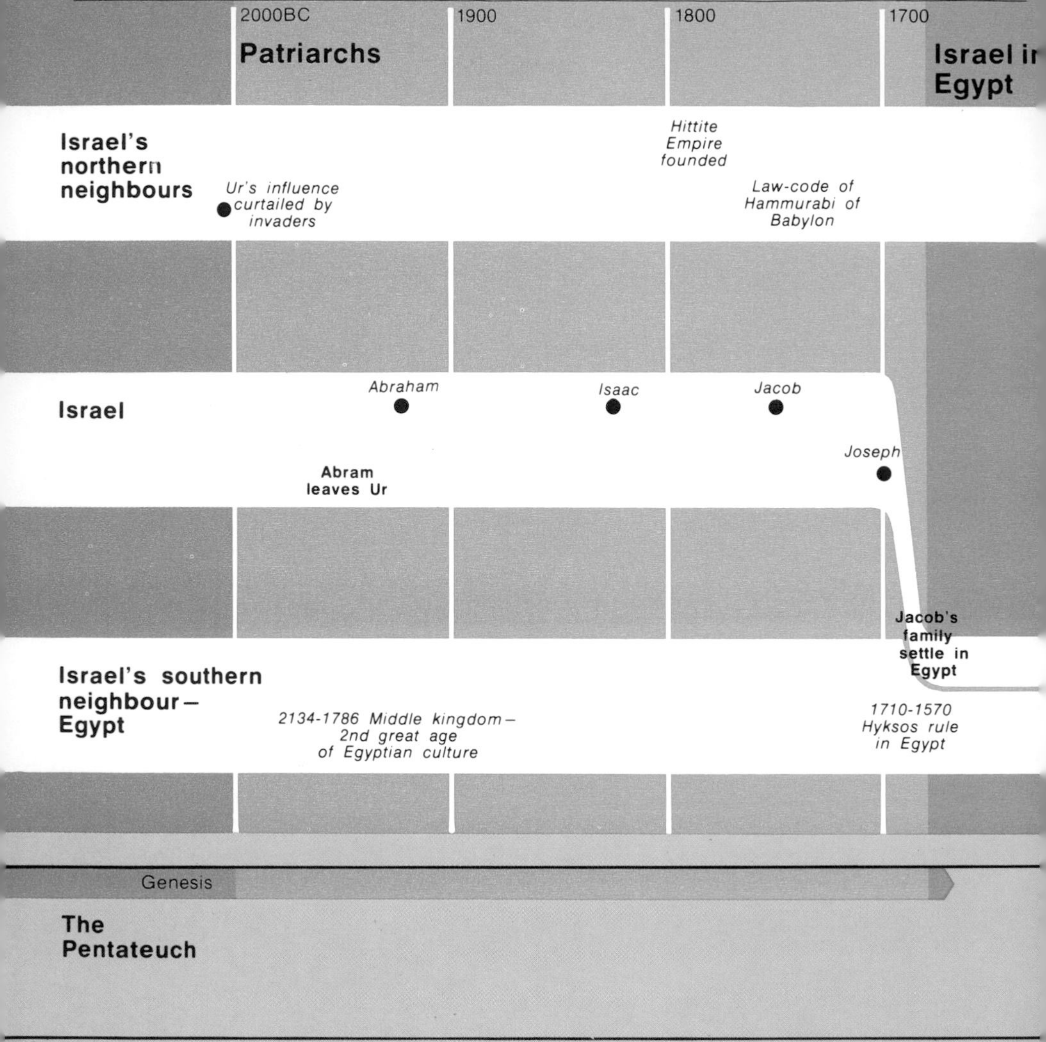

	2000BC	1900	1800	1700
	Patriarchs			**Israel in Egypt**

Israel's northern neighbours

● Ur's influence curtailed by invaders

Hittite Empire founded

Law-code of Hammurabi of Babylon

Israel

Abraham ●

Isaac ●

Jacob ●

Joseph ●

Abram leaves Ur

Jacob's family settle in Egypt

Israel's southern neighbour — Egypt

2134-1786 Middle kingdom — 2nd great age of Egyptian culture

1710-1570 Hyksos rule in Egypt

Genesis

The Pentateuch

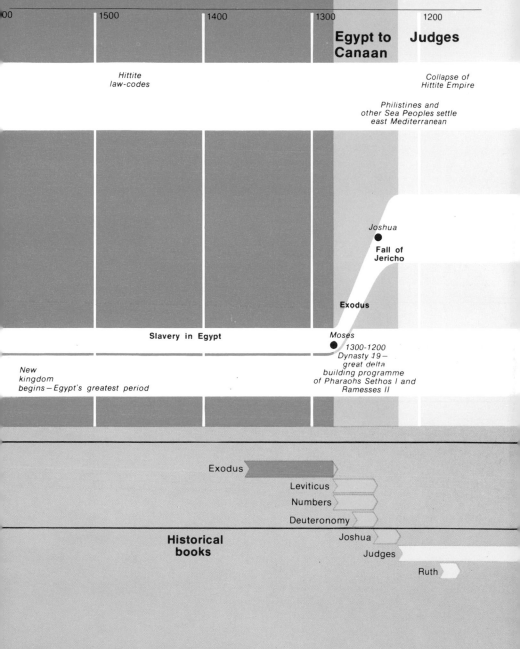

	1500	1400	1300	1200

Egypt to Canaan   **Judges**

Hittite law-codes

Collapse of Hittite Empire

Philistines and other Sea Peoples settle east Mediterranean

Joshua
●
Fall of Jericho

Exodus

Slavery in Egypt

Moses
●
1300-1200 Dynasty 19 — great delta building programme of Pharaohs Sethos I and Ramesses II

New kingdom begins — Egypt's greatest period

Exodus

Leviticus

Numbers

Deuteronomy

Historical books

Joshua

Judges

Ruth

OLD TESTAMENT HISTORY AT A GLANCE

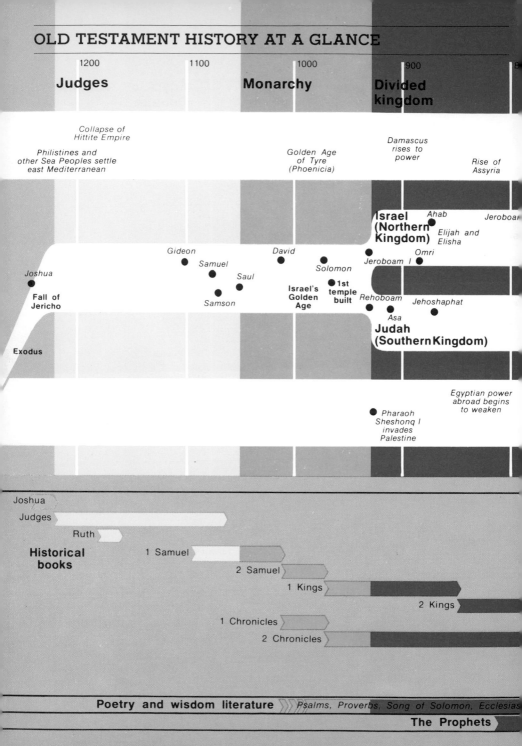

	1200	1100	1000	900	8
Judges			**Monarchy**	**Divided kingdom**	

Collapse of
Hittite Empire

Philistines and
other Sea Peoples settle
east Mediterranean

Golden Age
of Tyre
(Phoenicia)

Damascus
rises to
power

Rise of
Assyria

**Israel
(Northern
Kingdom)**

Ahab Jeroboa

Elijah and
Elisha

Omri

David

Gideon

Samuel

Solomon

Jeroboam I

Saul

Joshua

Samson

Israel's
Golden
Age

● 1st
temple
built

Rehoboam

Jehoshaphat

**Fall of
Jericho**

Asa

**Judah
(Southern Kingdom)**

Exodus

Egyptian power
abroad begins
to weaken

● Pharaoh
Sheshonq I
invades
Palestine

Joshua

Judges

Ruth

**Historical
books**

1 Samuel

2 Samuel

1 Kings

2 Kings

1 Chronicles

2 Chronicles

Poetry and wisdom literature 〉〉〉 *Psalms, Proverbs, Song of Solomon, Ecclesias*

The Prophets 〉

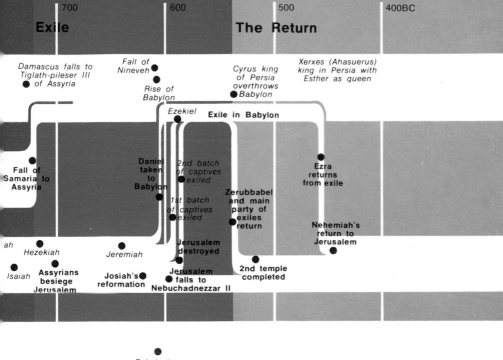

700   600   500   400BC

Exile   The Return

Damascus falls to
Tiglath-pileser III
● of Assyria

Fall of
Nineveh ●

Rise of
Babylon ●

Cyrus king
of Persia
overthrows
● Babylon

Xerxes (Ahasuerus)
king in Persia with
Esther as queen

Ezekiel   **Exile in Babylon**

Fall of
Samaria to
Assyria

Daniel
taken
to
Babylon ●

*2nd batch
of captives
● exiled*

Ezra
returns
from exile ●

*1st batch
of captives
● exiled*

Zerubbabel
and main
party of
exiles
return ●

Nehemiah's
return to
Jerusalem ●

ah
Hezekiah

Jeremiah

Jerusalem
destroyed ●

Isaiah   Assyrians
besiege
Jerusalem ●

Josiah's ●
reformation

Jerusalem
falls to ●
Nebuchadnezzar II

2nd temple
completed ●

●
*Babylonians
defeat Necho at
Carchemish*

Ezra ⟩

Nehemiah ⟩

Esther ⟩

⟩⟩⟩

See Prophets chart)

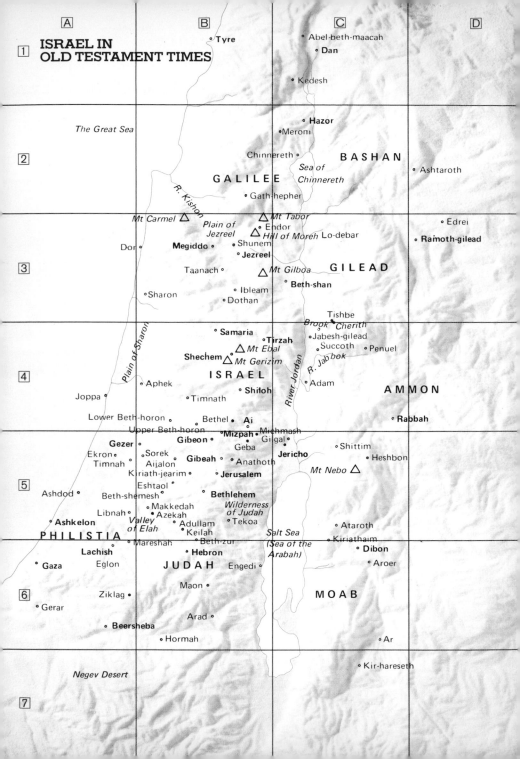

ISRAEL IN OLD TESTAMENT TIMES

A   **B**   **C**   **D**

1

° Tyre

° Abel-beth-maacah

• **Dan**

° Kedesh

2

The Great Sea

• **Hazor**
° Merom

Chinnereth °

BASHAN

Sea of Chinnereth

° **Ashtaroth**

GALILEE

R. Kishon

° Gath-hepher

3

Mt Carmel △

△ *Mt Tabor*

° Edrei

Plain of Jezreel

° Endor

△ *Hill of Moreh* Lo-debar

° **Ramoth-gilead**

Dor °

Megiddo °

° Shunem

• **Jezreel**

Taanach °

△ *Mt Gilboa*

GILEAD

° Sharon

° Ibleam

° Dothan

• **Beth-shan**

Tishbe °

Brook • *Cherith*

° Jabesh-gilead

4

° **Samaria**

• **Tirzah**

° Succoth

° Penuel

△ *Mt Ebal*

Shechem °

△ *Mt Gerizim*

R. Jabbok

ISRAEL

° Aphek

• **Shiloh**

° Adam

AMMON

Joppa °

° Timnath

Lower Beth-horon °

Bethel °

Ai •

Upper Beth-horon °

• **Rabbah**

• **Mizpah** • Michmash

Gezer °

Gibeon °

• Gilgal

Ekron °

Geba °

° Shittim

Plain of Sharon

River Jordan

5

° Sorek

Gibeah °

Jericho

° Heshbon

Timnah °

° Anathoth

Kiriath-jearim °

• **Jerusalem**

Mt Nebo △

Ashdod °

Eshtaol °

Beth-shemesh °

• **Bethlehem**

° Ataroth

Libnah °

Makkedah °

Wilderness of Judah

° Azekah

° **Ashkelon**

Valley of Elah

Adullam °

° Tekoa

° Kiriathaim

PHILISTIA

Keilah °

Salt Sea (Sea of the Arabah)

Mareshah °

° Beth-zur

• **Dibon**

Lachish °

• **Hebron**

Engedi °

° Aroer

° **Gaza**

Eglon °

JUDAH

6

Maon °

MOAB

Ziklag °

° Gerar

Arad °

• **Beersheba**

° Hormah

° Ar

7

Negev Desert

° Kir-hareseth

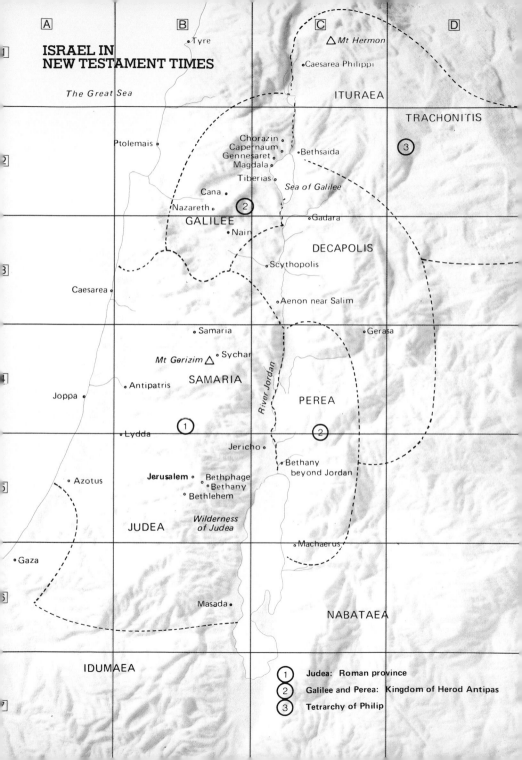

ISRAEL IN NEW TESTAMENT TIMES

A | B | C | D

1

The Great Sea

• Tyre

△ *Mt Hermon*

• Caesarea Philippi

ITURAEA

TRACHONITIS

2

Ptolemais •

Chorazin •
Capernaum •
Gennesaret •
Magdala •

• Bethsaida

③

Tiberias •

Sea of Galilee

Cana •

Nazareth •

②

GALILEE

• Gadara

• Nain

DECAPOLIS

3

Caesarea •

Scythopolis •

Aenon near Salim •

• Samaria

• Gerasa

Mt Gerizim △ • Sychar

4

SAMARIA

• Antipatris

Joppa •

River Jordan

PEREA

①

• Lydda

②

Jericho •

• Bethany
beyond Jordan

5

• Azotus

Jerusalem •

• Bethphage
• Bethany
• Bethlehem

JUDEA

*Wilderness
of Judea*

• Gaza

• Machaerus

6

Masada •

NABATAEA

7

IDUMAEA

① Judea: Roman province
② Galilee and Perea: Kingdom of Herod Antipas
③ Tetrarchy of Philip

NEW TESTAMENT HISTORY AT A GLANCE

Many New Testament dates, especially for the letters, are very approximate

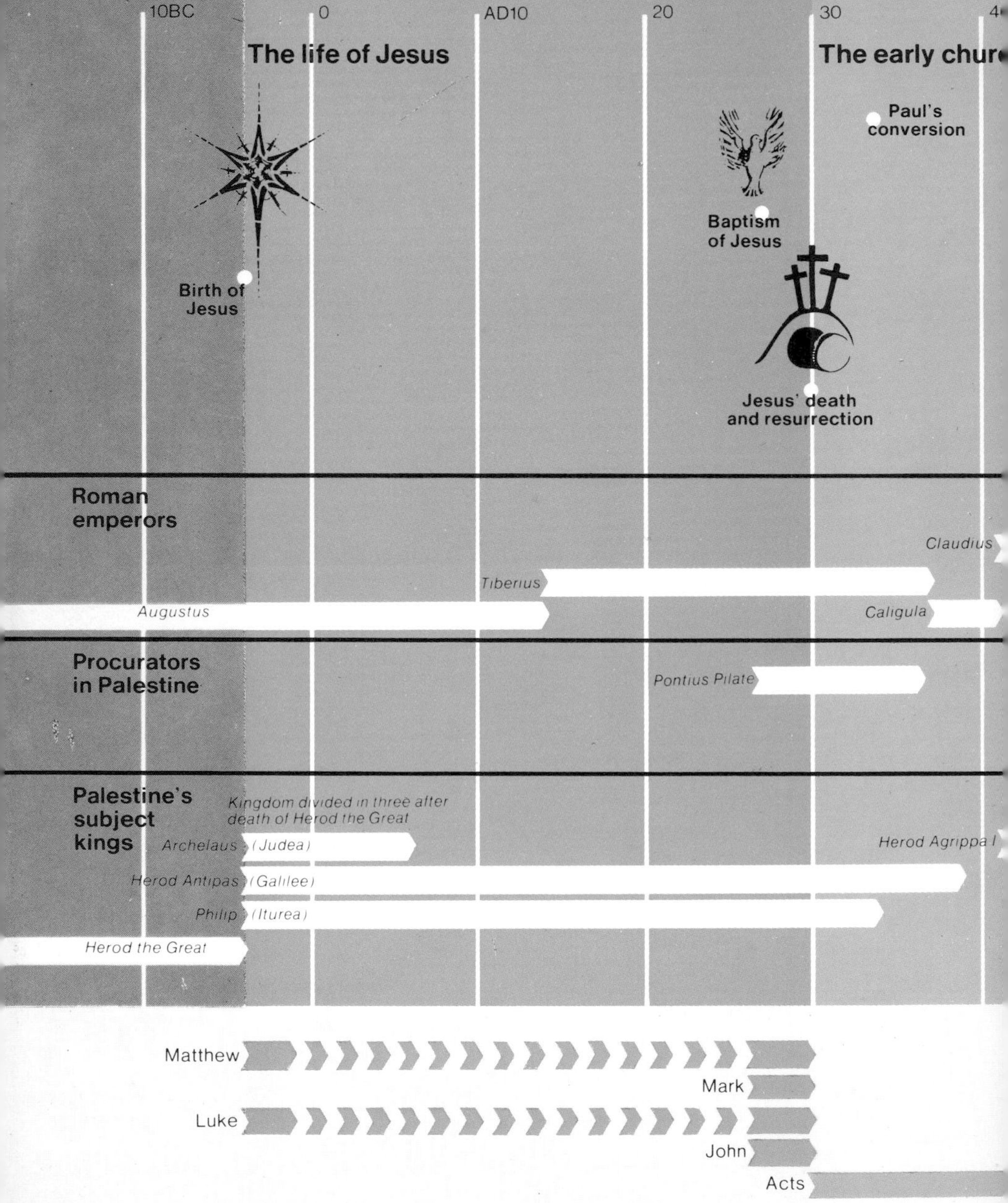

10BC	0	AD10	20	30	4

The life of Jesus

The early chur

Paul's conversion

Baptism of Jesus

Birth of Jesus

Jesus' death and resurrection

Roman emperors

Claudius

Tiberius

Augustus

Caligula

Procurators in Palestine

Pontius Pilate

Palestine's subject kings

Kingdom divided in three after death of Herod the Great

Archelaus (Judea)

Herod Agrippa I

Herod Antipas (Galilee)

Philip (Iturea)

Herod the Great

Matthew

Mark

Luke

John

Acts

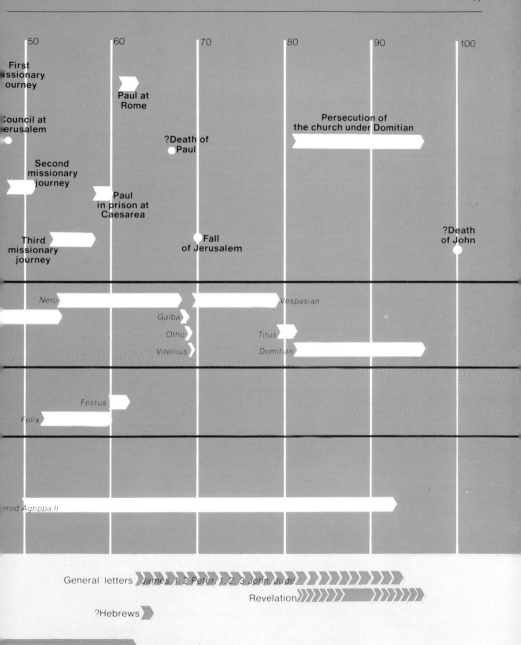

50   60   70   80   90   100

First
missionary
journey

Paul at
Rome

Council at
Jerusalem

Persecution of
the church under Domitian

?Death of
Paul

Second
missionary
journey

Paul
in prison at
Caesarea

?Death
of John

Third
missionary
journey

Fall
of Jerusalem

Nero   Vespasian

Galba

Otho   Titus

Vitellius   Domitian

Festus

Felix

Herod Agrippa II

General letters *James, 1, 2 Peter, 1, 2, 3 John, Jude*

Revelation

?Hebrews

Paul's letters

Mark

Matthew is formal and stately. Mark is bustling with life; full of action. Matthew collects Jesus' sayings. Mark concentrates on the marvellous things Jesus did, and the places he went to.

This is the shortest of the Gospels, and probably the first to be written (AD 65-70 or even earlier). There is a strong early tradition that John Mark wrote it in Rome, setting down Jesus' story as he had heard it direct from the apostle Peter. This would certainly account for the Gospel's extraordinary vividness. And Mark often explains Jewish customs, so he obviously had non-Jewish readers in mind.

He tells the story roughly in the order things happened – moving swiftly through from Jesus' baptism to the critical events of the cross and resurrection. Within this framework the material tends to be grouped by subject. Only four paragraphs in these 16 chapters are unique to Mark. All the rest appears again in either Matthew or Luke, or both. Yet to lose Mark would be to lose something beyond price. In Mark we see Jesus in action. And as we watch, the things he does convince us that he is the Son of God himself.

The writer

The name 'John Mark' occurs often in Acts and the epistles ('John' the Jewish name, 'Mark' the Latin). His mother had a house in Jerusalem where the early church met (Acts 12:12). And he was cousin to Paul's companion, Barnabas. Mark blotted his copybook with Paul by going home half-way through the first missionary tour. But Barnabas gave him a second chance, and he later won the love and respect of Paul and of Peter. He was a real comfort to Paul in prison (Colossians 4). And Peter, whose companion he became, loved him as his own son (1 Peter 5:13).

1:1-13
THE GOOD NEWS OF JESUS

1:1-8 John the Baptist

See also Matthew 3:1-12; Luke 3:2-22, and map. Mark passes over Jesus' birth. For him the good news begins with John, the voice Isaiah had predicted, crying out from the desert, urging the nation to make ready for God's coming. The rest of his account will show that Jesus is the Messiah – the one whose coming John announced – and Son of God.

Verses 2-3: Mark, like Matthew, combines Old Testament references: Exodus 23:20; Malachi 3:1; Isaiah 40:3.

Verse 8: water is a symbol. It can only clean the outside. The Holy Spirit can clean heart and mind and will.

The prophet from the desert: the 'wilderness' or desert-country around Jericho and south of Jerusalem is rough and uninviting. Scarcely anything grows: it is empty of human habitation, occupied only by wild animals. No doubt the very loneliness of the place, and the freedom from distraction, made it the ideal training-ground for John. Paul, too, was prepared for his mission during a time in the desert. There seems to be something in the stark simplicity of desert life which puts men – some men at least – in close touch with God. In the harsh sunlight there is only black or white, no shades of grey. It afforded John no other luxuries – only the simplest of food and rough clothing. His camel-hair tunic and leather belt may have been worn in conscious imitation of Elijah (see 2 Kings 1:8 and the prophecy in Malachi 4:5). He was certainly recognized instantly as a prophet. He not only looked the part, he possessed the prophet's cast-iron assurance that he had a God-given message to proclaim. The people flocked from far and wide to hear him, probably gathering beside the Jordan

The Jordan river, where John baptized, winds from the Lake of Galilee, well below sea level, down through the semi-tropical rift-valley to the Dead Sea.

near Jericho, close to the place where Joshua had crossed into the promised land so many centuries before.

1:9-13 Jesus' baptism and temptation

See on Matthew 3-4; Luke 3:21; 4:1-13. Mark gives only a brief résumé.

1:14—9:50
JESUS IN GALILEE

The Roman province of Galilee, under Herod's jurisdiction, lay to the west of the Sea of Galilee. We tend to think of it as a remote country district. But in Christ's day the region was prosperous and densely populated, criss-crossed by Roman military roads and ancient trade routes – north, south, east and west. The fresh-water Lake of Galilee – 13 miles/ 21 km long, 7 miles/11 km wide, sunk in the deep trough of the Jordan rift valley over 600 feet/180 metres below sea-level – is the focal point in Jesus' travels. It divided Herod's territory from that of his half-brother Philip, to the east. Most of the apostles came from the towns around the lake-shore which enjoyed a sub-tropical climate. Capernaum was Jesus' base. Tiberias, 10 miles/16 km away, was a spa town famous for its hot baths. Many of the sick people Jesus healed must have come to the area for the mineral waters at Tiberias. On the hill behind the town was Herod's splendid summer palace. The lake is ringed round with hills – brown and barren on the east; in those days green, fertile, wooded on the west. Over the tops, and funnelling down through them, races the wind that can whip the lake into a sudden fury of storm. North, the snow-capped summit of Mt Hermon dominates the skyline – the mount of the transfiguration. In Jesus' day palms, olives, figs and vines grew on the hillsides round the lake. And the little towns and villages on its western shore were thriving centres of industry – fish pickled for export; boat-building; dye-works; potteries. John the Baptist lived an ascetic life in the desert. By contrast, Jesus chose to be in the thick of things, in Galilee, one of the busiest, most cosmopolitan regions of Palestine.

1:14-20 Jesus calls his first disciples

John's voice is silenced. Jesus travels north again, and begins his own public proclamation of God's good news. By the Lake of Galilee he calls his first disciples – all of them fishermen. (John 1:35-42 fills in the background.)

1:21-45 Jesus begins to teach and heal

From now on Capernaum is Jesus' headquarters. His teaching in the synagogue and his handling of the possessed man both convey an extra-ordinary *authority.*

Again and again, as in the case of the leper here, Mark stresses Jesus' insist-ence on *secrecy.* The people were expecting the Messiah to be a political leader. News of Jesus' amazing powers, which marked him out as the Messiah, could easily have sparked off a rising against the Roman occupation. It was imperative the miracles should be accompanied by teaching to explain the kind of 'kingdom' Jesus had come to inaugurate, and the Messiah's real mission.

Verse 32: at sunset the sabbath was over, and restrictions on movement no longer applied.

Verse 44: see Leviticus 14:1-32. In the Bible, the term 'leprosy' covers a variety of skin diseases.

At Capernaum the local Roman centurion had contributed to the building of the synagogue. The ruins of the Capernaum synagogue pictured here (probably built two or three centuries later) show a combination of Roman style and traditional Jewish symbols.

2:1-12 The paralytic walks

It is easy enough simply to tell a man his sins are forgiven. But by healing him Jesus visibly demonstrates his power in both physical and spiritual realms. When he says the word, something really happens.

Verse 4: the house would have an outside staircase leading to a flat roof, giving extra living-space. The roof would be made of tiles or lath and plaster – not difficult to break through.

Verse 11: ordinary people slept on the floor on a mat or bedding which could be rolled up in the daytime.

2:13-22 Levi (Matthew) becomes a disciple; the question of fasting

See on Matthew 9:9-17; Luke 5:27-39.
Scribes, Pharisees (16): see page 494.

2:23 — 3:6 The purpose of the sabbath; opposition

See also Matthew 12:1-14; Luke 6:1-11. Jewish interpretation of the fourth commandment (Exodus 20:8-11; 34:21) had hedged it about with so many petty rules and restrictions that its primary purpose was lost. The day of rest was intended for man's physical and spiritual good, not to deny him food and help. It is a day for doing good – and not only in an emergency.

2:25-26: see 1 Samuel 21:1-6. The loaves David took were those the priests placed each week on the altar.

Herodians (3:6): supporters of Herod Antipas, see page 540. They collaborated with the Romans, and were therefore normally abhorrent to the scrupulous Pharisees.

3:7-19 The Twelve

Crowds flock to Jesus from the south (Judea, Jerusalem, Idumaea); from the east across the Jordan; and from Tyre and Sidon, the coastal towns in the north-west. See map.

Jesus chose an inner circle of 12 disciples who became founder-members of the new kingdom – the counterparts of Jacob's 12 sons, who gave their names to the tribes of Israel. Three – Peter, James and John – were specially close to him. Four of the Twelve, all from Galilee, were partners in a fishing business (Peter and his brother Andrew; James and his brother John). One (Matthew/Levi, who may have been the brother of James son of Alphaeus) was a tax collector, serving the Romans. Simon, at the other end of the scale, belonged to an extremist guerilla group (the Zealots) working to overthrow the occupation. We know little of the others. The full list also appears in Matthew 10:2-4 and Luke 6:12-16. The 'Thaddaeus' of Matthew and Mark seems to be the same as 'Judas son of James' (Luke, Acts 1:13). Bartholomew is often identified with the Nathanael of John 1. They were certainly a very mixed bunch of men.

Verse 12: see on 1:21-45

3:20-35 Suspicion and accusation

See on Matthew 12:15-37 and 49.

4:1-34 Jesus teaches in parables

See on Matthew 13:1-52.
Verses 1-25: the seed and the soils.
Verses 26-29: the wheat and the weeds.
Verses 30-32: the mustard-seed.

Verse 12: in Jewish idiom, result is often expressed as if it were intention. This verse refers to the 'consequence', not the 'purpose' of Christ's teaching. It is clear from verses 22-23 that the reason for wrapping up the meaning is to encourage the listener to search it out for himself.

4:35-41 Jesus calms the great storm

Sudden storms sometimes whip the Lake of Galilee into fury (see page 500). Jesus has power to control the elements.

5:1-20 Across the lake; the man possessed by demons

See also Matthew 8:28-34; Luke 8:26-39. The man is a pitiful sight – a fragmented personality at the mercy of a hundred conflicting impulses; totally incapable of a normal life. Is any greater contrast imaginable than the description of 2-5 and verse 15? Jesus had power not only over nature but also over human nature; and not only over human nature but over the spiritual forces of evil.

Region of the Gerasenes (1): the general area south-east of the lake. At only one point on the eastern bank is there a steep slope (13).

Decapolis (20): 'Ten Towns'; ten free Greek cities.

5:21-43 Jairus' daughter restored to life; the woman with the haemorrhage

See also Matthew 9:18-26; Luke 8:40-56.

The woman tries not to advertise her presence, because the haemorrhage makes her polluted and untouchable to her fellow Jews. There is no magic about Jesus' clothes. He knows the difference between the casual contact of the crowd and someone reaching out in need. The incident must have encouraged Jairus. The fact that he came to Jesus shows that not all religious leaders were against him.

Verse 39: this was not just a coma – the child really was dead. Everyone knew it (40). Jesus' words describe death as God sees it – a sleep from which we wake to a new day.

6:1-13 In and around Nazareth; the Twelve sent out

Verses 1-6: in Jesus' home town it is not a case of 'local boy makes good' but 'who does this jumped-up carpenter think he is?' It was not in line with Jesus' purpose to make a display of his powers in order to convince sceptics (see Matthew 4:6-7).

Verses 7-13: see on Matthew 9:35-10:42.
Verse 3: see on Matthew 12:49. James later became the leader of the church in Jerusalem (Acts 15:13). Judas wrote the Epistle of Jude.

Five loaves and two small fish. These fish from the Lake of Galilee are known as St Peter's Fish, as their large mouths, in which they carry their eggs, could hold a coin (see Matthew 17:27). The fish in the story of the feeding of the 5,000 may have been pickled rather than fresh.

6:14-29 Herod and John the Baptist

Guilt and superstition make Herod think Jesus is John come to life again. Herod had divorced his own wife to marry Herodias, wife of his half-brother Philip. John had denounced this as incest (Leviticus 18:16; 20:21), and been imprisoned for his pains. According to Josephus his prison was the fortress of Machaerus in the far south, east of the Dead Sea. But Herodias wanted to still the preacher's tongue permanently.

6:30-44 5,000 miraculously fed

See also Matthew 14:13-21; Luke 9:10b-17; John 6:5-14. John's death casts a shadow. Jesus is desperately tired and hard-pressed.

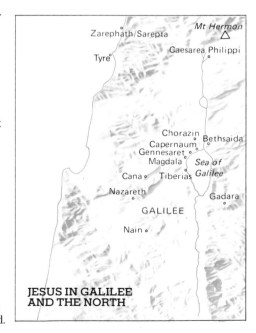

JESUS IN GALILEE AND THE NORTH

Yet instead of being annoyed or irritable with the pursuing crowds, his heart goes out to them.

Verse 37: needless to say they did not have this kind of money: the denarius 'silver coin' was a working man's wage for the day–this would be over six months' wages.

6:45-56 Jesus walks on the lake

It was some time between 3 a.m. and 6 a.m. Again it is the disciples' need that calls out Jesus' love. And again he demonstrates his supreme power over creation: he is Lord of wind and water.
Fringe/edge (56): the blue-tasselled border of his cloak. See page 90.

7:1-23 The Pharisees and their traditions

See on Matthew 15:1-20. Mark adds an explanatory note for non-Jewish readers (3-4). The Pharisees were concerned not with hygiene but with religious 'cleanness'. Man's real problem is not dirty hands but a polluted heart, which no amount of washing can clean. Jesus exposes their wrong thinking.

Sunrise over Mt Hermon, probable site of the transfiguration of Jesus.

7:24-37 The Greek woman's daughter; the deaf mute

Verses 24-30: see on Matthew 15:21-28.

Verses 31-37: the man's speech defect, as so often, was the result of his deafness. Saliva was popularly thought to have healing power.

8:1-21 4,000 fed; the demand for a sign; the 'yeast' of the Pharisees

Verses 1-9; see on Matthew 15:29-39. Dalmanutha is not known.

Verses 11-21: see on Matthew 16:1-12. The disciples lack spiritual discernment. They are so taken up with the bread-supply that they cannot see that Jesus is warning them against the ever-present danger of religious hypocrisy (see Luke 12:1) and materialism (the prime concern of the pro-Herod faction).

8:22-26 A blind man regains his sight

Jesus once again guards against publicity – see on 1:21-45.

8:27–9:1 'Who do men say I am?'; Jesus predicts his death

See on Matthew 16:13-28. Here and elsewhere Mark records in full incidents which show Peter's failings, but plays down the credit side–understandable if the information came from Peter himself. This episode is a pivotal point in the story. From now on, Jesus stresses the suffering which lies ahead.
Caesarea Philippi (27): 25 miles/40 km north of the Lake of Galilee. See map.
9:1: see on Matthew 10:23.

9:2-13 The disciples see Jesus transfigured

See also Matthew 17:1-13; Luke 9:28-36. The apostles are sure now that Jesus is the Messiah. This special glimpse of his glory, given to the inner three, must have been tremendously reassuring through all that lay ahead. Moses (Israel's great lawgiver) and Elijah (the first great prophet) converse with Jesus about his coming death (Luke 9:31).

Verse 2: the mountain is believed to be 9,000 foot/2,700 m Mt Hermon as it is only 12 miles/19 km north-east of Caesarea Philippi. The tradition that it was Mt Tabor does not fit the geography so well. Peter wants to prolong the present moment. Perhaps Moses and Elijah will stay if they make shelters for them, like the tent (tabernacle) where God was present in the old days, before the temple was built. The glory of all he saw that day imprinted itself indelibly on Peter's memory (2 Peter 1:16-18).

Verse 13: 'Elijah', i.e. John the Baptist (see Matthew 17:13). Malachi (4:5) had predicted a reappearance of Elijah to announce the day of God's coming.

9:14-29 The epileptic boy

See also Matthew 17:14-19; Luke 9:37-42. The disciples fail because of their lack of faith (see Matthew 17:19-20). Yet Jesus will accept even a grain of faith in him (24). He does not wait to heal the child until the father's faith is greater.

9:30-50 Status and Christian responsibility

See on Matthew 18. No one who is preoccupied with selfish ambition can become a 'great' Christian. It has to be other people first, self last. Today we lay great stress on self-fulfilment and the full development of personality. Jesus puts this in perspective. It is better deliberately to limit that fulfilment, to handicap ourselves in this life (44-45) than miss God's kingdom altogether.

Verses 43-48: Jesus draws his terrible picture of hell from Jerusalem's permanently smouldering refuse-tip in the valley of Hinnom (Gehenna), and the dead bodies gradually eaten away by worms.

Verse 49: 'Salted with fire'–i.e. purified in the 'refinery' of suffering (see Good News Bible).

10

ON THE WAY TO JERUSALEM

10:1-12 Divorce
See on Matthew 19:1-15.

10:13-16 Jesus blesses the children

To enter God's kingdom we must all become, not childish, but childlike– receiving him with humble, loving trust (15).

10:17-31 The positive disadvantage of wealth

See on Matthew 19:16-30; Luke 18:18-30. This incident does not imply that all Christ's followers must become penni- less. He is speaking to one man, not to all, and in this case the man's possessions kept him from becoming a disciple. Anything that takes first place–God's place–in our lives must go. So Jesus tells him, 'Go, sell' *and* 'Come, follow me'.

10:32-45 Jesus again predicts his death; the disciples bicker over their future status

See on Matthew 20:17-34.

10:46-52 Blind Bartimaeus

See also Matthew 20:29-34 (where there are two men); Luke 18:35-43. Only Mark tells us the beggar's name. As he afterwards joined the company of Jesus' followers, Peter presumably came to know him.

11–13

JESUS IN JERUSALEM

11:1-11 The triumphant entry

See introduction to Matthew 21; and see on Luke 19:28-44.

11:12-26 The fig-tree; the purging of the temple

See on Matthew 21:18-22 and 12-17.

11:27 – 12:12 The religious leaders question Jesus' authority; the parable of the vineyard

See on Matthew 21:23-46.

12:13-44 Test questions; Jesus in the temple

See also Matthew 22:15-46; Luke 20:19–21:4. Luke 20:19-20 gives the background to these questions.

Verses 13-17: there was little love lost between the strictly religious Pharisees and the opportunist Herodians. But they join forces to try to trap Jesus into a treasonable statement.

Verses 18-27: the blinkered Sadducees try to ridicule the idea of resurrection with an absurd case of Levirate marriage (see page 226). But the laugh is on them, because there *is* a resurrection – to a life where there is no sexual union or procreation because there is no death.

Verses 28-34: the third question is a genuine one. With 613 commandments to choose from, Jesus replies in the words of Israel's creed (the Shema; Deuteronomy 6:4-5) and Leviticus 19:18. If the Pharisees hoped for an unorthodox reply (Matthew 22:34-35) they were disappointed. The astonishing wisdom of Jesus silences his opponents – but *he*

has not finished with *them* (35-40).

In strong contrast to the self-advertisement of the men of religion comes the little incident in verses 41-44. What counts with God is not the size of the cheque, but the amount of love and self-sacrifice it represents.

13 Judgement on Jerusalem: Jesus speaks about his return

See on Matthew 24. See also Luke 21 and 17:22ff.

14 – 16
JESUS' DEATH AND RESURRECTION

14:1-11 The plot against his life; the costly flask of perfume; betrayal

See also Matthew 26:6-13; John 12:1-8. Jesus' public ministry is at an end. As the Passover festival approaches (see on Matthew 26) events move swiftly to a climax. Against a dark backcloth of hatred and treachery shines the story of one woman's love for the Lord (3-9). Perhaps intuitively sensing the tragedy ahead, Mary (see John 12:3) pours out the precious perfumed oil in a lavish, extravagant gesture of affection. (A working man earned one denarius/'silver coin' a day. This luxury import was

An alabaster flask, like Mary's, inscribed 'cinnamon'; Hellenistic, from Egypt.

worth nearly a year's wages.) John (12:1-8) places the event some days earlier and tells us the unpleasant truth about Judas' embezzlement of the funds. In Luke 7:36-50 the occasion is similar, but the woman concerned different.

14:12-25 The Last Supper
See on Matthew 26:14-29.

14:26-52 Gethsemane; Jesus is arrested
See on Matthew 26:30-56. There seems little point in the mention of the young man (51-62) unless this is Mark himself.

14:53 — 15:15 The Jewish trial; Peter denies Jesus; the Roman trial

See on Luke 22:54-71.

The trials
The Jewish court which tried Jesus was the Sanhedrin, the supreme court at Jerusalem. Its 71 councillors came from influential families – elders, lawyers, Pharisees and Sadducees. The high priest for the year presided. The Sanhedrin had wide powers in civil and religious matters in Judea, but under Roman rule was not empowered to carry out the death sentence. So Jesus had also to appear before the Roman governor on a charge which would merit the death sentence under Roman law. Blasphemy was sufficient for the Jews. To be sure Pilate would ratify the sentence, the safest charge was treason. The Jewish trial was far from regular. It was held at night. There were no defence witnesses. The witnesses for the prosecution could not agree. And the death sentence, which should not have been pronounced till the day following the trial (the Jewish day ran from sunset to sunset), was immediate.

The sequence of events
1. The audience with Annas, father-in-law of high priest Caiaphas (John 18:12-14).

The traditional site of the crucifixion, the 'Place of a Skull', is marked by the Church of the Holy Sepulchre. It was General Gordon in the last century who suggested that this rocky outcrop outside the walls of the Old City of Jerusalem bore a striking resemblance to a skull, and could be the place where Jesus died.

2. The late-night session at Caiaphas' house before the Sanhedrin (Matthew 26:57-68; Mark 15:53-65; Luke 22:54-65; John 18:24).
3. The early morning ratification of the sentence by the Sanhedrin (Matthew 27:1; Mark 15:1; Luke 22:66-71).
4. Jesus before Pilate (Matthew 27:2, 11-14; Mark 15:2-5; Luke 23:1-5; John 18:28-38).
5. Since Jesus is a Galilean, Pilate refers him to Herod (Luke 23:6-12).
6. Jesus before Pilate again. He is scourged, sentenced and handed over to the soldiers (Matthew 27:15-26; Mark 15:6-15; Luke 23:13-25; John 18:29–19:16).

15: 16-41 Mockery and crucifixion

Jesus is now utterly alone. The Gospel writers play down the physical horror of the six hours (9 a.m.-3 p.m.) on the cross when Jesus touched a depth of suffering in body, mind and spirit beyond the stretch of our imagination. But the whole New Testament declares that his suffering was 'for us'. By his death he paid in full the penalty for our sin. He saved us from the death sentence, making possible the free gift of eternal life.

Seven times in those six hours (the last three in darkness) those who watched heard him speak.

Verse 21: Cyrene in north Africa had a strong Jewish colony. Alexander and Rufus evidently became Christians. This may be the same Rufus as the one mentioned in Romans 16:13.

Salome (40): Zebedee's wife; mother of James and John (Matthew 27:56).

15: 42-47 Burial

Death by crucifixion was long drawn out. It often took two days or more. But Jesus was dead in six hours. Joseph saves him from the final indignity of a mass grave.

Preparation Day (42): i.e. the day before the sabbath, which began at 6 p.m.

16 The resurrection

See on Luke 24. For some unknown reason – most probably damage to very early copies of the Gospel – the best manuscripts we have of Mark end abruptly at 16:8. Verses 9-20 represent early attempts to round the Gospel off more satisfactorily.

The words from the cross

1. *'Father, forgive them; for they do not know what they are doing'* (Luke 23:34)
– a prayer for the Jewish people and the Roman soldiers.

2. *'I tell you the truth, today you will be with me in paradise'* (Luke 23:43)
– his word to the repentant thief, crucified beside him.

3. *'Woman, here is your son!' 'Here is your mother!'* (John 19:26-27)
– commending his mother to John's care.

4. *'My God, my God, why have you forsaken me?'* (Matthew 27:46; Mark 15:34)
– expressing in the words of Psalm 22:1 the agony of separation from God as the full weight of human sin pressed upon him.

5. *'I am thirsty'* (John 19:28).

6. *'It is finished'* (John 19:30).

7. *'Father, into your hands I commit my spirit!'* (Luke 23:46).

The body of Jesus was bound in linen cloths with spices and laid in a rock-cut tomb. This picture is of the Garden Tomb in Jerusalem.

Key Themes of the Bible

Passages of the Bible on key ideas or themes, selected as examples as a starting-point for study.

ATONEMENT God and man made 'at one' by the 'covering' of man's sin before God: Leviticus 4; 16; Romans 3:25; 1 John 2:2; 4:10. See also under Reconciliation and Redemption.

CHURCH The people of God: John 1:12-13; 1 Corinthians 12:12-31; 2 Corinthians 6:16-18; Galatians 3:6-29; Ephesians 2:11-22; Colossians 1:15-20; 1 Peter 2:4-10.
Its foundation: Matthew 16:18-20; 28:16-20; John 10:7-18; Acts 1:6-8; 2.
Its mission and purpose: Matthew 28:19-20; John 17:18. 22ff.; Acts 1:8; 26:16-18; 2 Corinthians 5:18-21; Ephesians 3:7-13; 5:25-27; Philippians 1:5-11; 1 Peter 2:5, 9; Jude 24-25.
Unity: John 17; 1 Corinthians 1:10ff.; 11:17ff.; Galatians 1:6-9; 3:23-29; Ephesians 4; 1 Peter 3:8ff.
Leadership: Acts 6:1-6; 13:1-3; 14:21-23; 20:17-35; 1 Corinthians 12:4-30; 1 Thessalonians 5:12-13; 1 Timothy; Titus; Hebrews 13:17.
Gatherings: Acts 2:41-47; 11:19-26; 19:8-10; 20:7-12; 1 Corinthians 11:17-33; 14:26-39; Hebrews 10:23-25.
Discipline: Matthew 18:15-20; Acts 4:33 - 5:11; 1 Corinthians 5; 2 Corinthians 2:5-11; Galatians 6:1-3; 1 Timothy 5:17-22.
Message: see Gospel.

COVENANT A 'treaty' or 'agreement' setting out God's promises to man (see too special article pp.198-199, and pp.134, 164-165):
With Noah: Genesis 6:18; 9:9-17.
With Abraham: Genesis 15; 17.
With Israel: Exodus 19ff.; Deuteronomy 4ff.
With David: 2 Samuel 7; Psalms 89; 132.
The 'new covenant': Jeremiah 31:31-34; Matthew 26:26-28; 2 Corinthians 3; Galatians 4:21ff.; Hebrews 9:15ff.

CREATION AND PROVIDENCE Genesis 1 - 2; Job 38 - 42:6; Psalms 8; 33:6-22; 104; Isaiah 40:21-26; Matthew 6:25-33; Acts 14:15-18; Romans 1:18-23; 8:18-23; 13:1-7; Colossians 1:15-20; Hebrews 1:1-3. For the new creation, see Life; for the new heaven and earth, see Heaven.

DEATH The physical and spiritual consequence of man's sin — alienation from God: Genesis 2:17; Romans 5:12ff.; 6:23; Ephesians 2:1-5.
Victory over death: John 5:24; 8:51; 11:25; Romans 5:17ff.; 6; 8:6-11, 38-39; 1 Corinthians 15:26, 54-56; 1 John 3:14; Revelation 21:4.
The 'second death': Revelation 2:11; 20:6. 14; 21:8.

ELECTION God's choice; his right to single people out for blessing (see too note, p.586): Romans 9:18ff.
God's choice of individuals for a particular purpose or job: Genesis 12:1-2; Exodus 3; 1 Samuel 3; Isaiah 6; 45; 49; Jeremiah 1.
God's choice of a people: Deuteronomy 7:6ff.; Romans 8:28-30; 1 Corinthians 1:27ff.; Ephesians 1:4-12; 1 Peter 1:2; 2:9.

FAITH *Trust in God; belief in his promises:* Genesis 15:6; Psalm 37:3ff.; Proverbs 3:5-6; Jeremiah 17:7-8.
A way of life: Habakkuk 2:4; Hebrews 11; James 2.
Commitment to Jesus Christ, trusting him for salvation: John 1:12; 8:24; Acts 16:30-31; Romans 1:16-17; 4; Galatians 3; Ephesians 2:8-9; 1 John 5:1-5.
The means of access to God's power: Matthew 17:20-21; Mark 9:23; James 5:13-18.

FLESH *Flesh and blood; mortal man:* Genesis 6:3, 12; Psalm 78:39; Job 19:26; 34; 15; Isaiah 40:5.
The sinful self: Romans 7:13-25; 8; Galatians 5:16-24.

FORGIVENESS God's loving mercy: Exodus 34:6-7; Psalm 51; Isaiah 55:6-7; 1 John 1:5-10.
The death of Christ as the basis of God's forgiveness: Matthew 26:26-28; John 1:29; Acts 5:31; 13:38; Ephesians 1:7; 1 John 2:2, 12.
Forgiving others: Matthew 6:14-15; 18:21-35; Ephesians 4:32; Colossians 3:13.

FREEDOM Isaiah 61:1; Luke 4:18; John 8:31-36; Romans 6:16-23; 8:2, 21; 2 Corinthians 3:17; Galatians 3:28; 5:1; 13; James 1:25; 2:12; 1 Peter 2:16.

FUTURE DESTINY The day is coming (Old Testament 'that day', the 'day of the Lord') when God will judge all men; when all his glorious promises to his people will be realized in a new heaven and earth (see also Heaven, Jesus Christ, return and Resurrection): Isaiah 2 - 4; 65:17-25, etc.; Daniel 12:1-3; Joel; Amos 5; Zephaniah; Matthew 24 - 25; Acts 1:6-11, 1 Corinthians 3:10-15; 1 Corinthians 15:20-28. 35-58; Revelation, especially 19 - 22.

GOD One God who has disclosed himself in three persons — Father, Son (Jesus Christ) and Holy Spirit: Deuteronomy 6:4; Genesis 1:1-2 and John 1:1-3; Judges 14:6. etc.; Isaiah 40:13; 45:18-22; 61:1; 63:10, etc.; Matthew 28:19; John 14:15-26; 2 Corinthians 13:14; Ephesians 2:18; 4:4-6; 2 Thessalonians 2:13-14; 1 Peter 1:1-2.

The 'otherness' of God: the eternal spirit; the creator: Genesis 1; Deuteronomy 33:26-27; 1 Kings 8:27; Job 38ff.; Psalms 8; 100; 104; Isaiah 40:12-28; 55:9; John 4:23-24; Romans 1:19-20; Revelation 1:8.
The power of God: Genesis 17:1; Exodus 32:11; Numbers 24:4; Job 40 - 42:2; Isaiah 9:6; 45 - 46; Daniel 3:17; Matthew 26:53; John 19:10-11; Acts 12; Revelation 19:1-16.
— his knowledge: Genesis 4:10; Job 28:20-27; Psalm 139:1-6; Daniel 2:17-23; Matthew 6:7-8; John 2:23-25; 4:25-29; Ephesians 1:3-12.
— his presence everywhere: Genesis 28:10-17; Psalm 139:7-12; Jeremiah 23:23-24; Acts 17:26-28.
The character of God — his holiness and righteousness: Exodus 20; Leviticus 11:44-45; Joshua 24:19-28; Psalms 7; 25:8-10; 99; Isaiah 1:12ff.; 6:1-5; John 17:25-26; Romans 1:18 - 3:26; Ephesians 4:17-24; Hebrews 12: 7-14; 1 Peter 1:13-16; 1 John 1:5-10.
— his love and mercy: Deuteronomy 7:6-13; Psalms, e.g., 23; 25; 36:5-12; 103; Isaiah 40:1-2, 27-31; 41:8-20; 43; Jeremiah 31:2-14; Hosea 6; 11; 14; John 3:16-17; 10:7-18; 13:1; 14:15-31; 15:9. 12ff.; Romans 8:35-38; Galatians 2:20; Ephesians 2:4-10; 1 John 3:1-3. 16; 4:7-21.

GOSPEL The 'good news' brought by Jesus: Mark 1:14-15; Luke 8:1; etc.
The gospel message: e.g. Matthew 4:17; John 1:11-13; 3:1-21. 31-36; Acts 2; 13; 17; 6:23). 2 Corinthians 5:17ff.; Galatians 2:20; 4:4-7; Ephesians 1:3ff.; 1 John 1:1-4; 5:11-12. See also Kingdom, Life, Salvation.

GRACE God's love poured out on undeserving man (the Old Testament uses a number of different terms): Deuteronomy 7:6-9; Psalms 23:6; 25:6-10; 51:1; Jeremiah 31:2-3.
God's grace in salvation: Ephesians 2:4-9; Romans 3:19-24; 6:14.
The Christian's dependence on God's grace: 2 Corinthians 12:9; Ephesians 4:7; 1 Timothy 1:2; 1 Peter 5:5. 10; 2 Peter 3:18.

HEAVEN The dwelling-place of God, the perfect, unseen world (also sometimes simply a word for 'sky'): Deuteronomy 26:15; Nehemiah 9:6; Matthew 5:45; 6:9; Mark 13:32; 1 Peter 1:4.
The 'new heaven and earth': Isaiah 65:17ff.; 2 Peter 3:10-13; Revelation 21 - 22.

HELL 'Sheol', Old Testament place of the dead (= New Testament 'Hades'): Psalms 88:3-5; 139:8; Proverbs 9:18; Isaiah 5:14; 38:18; Amos 9:2. New Testament 'Gehenna', the fate of those finally cut off from God: Matthew 5:22. 29-30; 10:28; 23:33; 25:41; 2 Peter 2:4; Revelation 1:18. 20:13-15.

HOLINESS God's moral perfection; his separation from evil and distinctive character: Exodus 3:4-6; 15:11; 1 Chronicles

16:10; Isaiah 6:3-5; 10:20; Hosea 11:9; John 17:11; Revelation 4:8.
Expressed in Jesus: Acts 4:27, 30; John 1:14-18; 14:6ff.
In God's people: Exodus 19:6; Luke 1:74-75; 2 Corinthians 7:1; Ephesians 4:23-24; Colossians 3:12ff.; Hebrews 12:10-11; 1 Peter 1:15-16; 2:9.

HOLY SPIRIT One with God the Father and Jesus Christ, actively at work in the world of men, particularly in and through God's people.
His nature and person: Genesis 1:1-2; 2 Samuel 23:2-5; Psalm 139:7-12; Matthew 12:25-32; 28:19; John 14:15-17; 15:26-27; Acts 5:1-3; 20:28; Romans 8:9-11; 2 Corinthians 3:15-18; 13:14; Ephesians 4:29-31.
His work: Exodus 31:3; Judges 3:10; 14:6, etc.; Psalm 51:10-12; Isaiah 11:1-3; 32:14-18; 42:1-4; 63:10-14; Ezekiel 36:26-27; John 3:5-8; 14:25-26; 16:7-15; Acts 1:6-8; 2:11:16-18; Romans 5:1-5; 8:1-27; 1 Corinthians 2:1-13; 12:3-13; 2 Corinthians 1:20-22; Galatians 5:16-25; 2 Peter 1:20-21.

HOPE Confident expectation: Romans 4:18; 5:1-5; 8:24-25; 12:12; 15:4; 1 Corinthians 13:13; 15:19ff.; Colossians 1:5, 27; 1 Peter 1:3ff.; Hebrews 11:1ff.

INCARNATION God become man: Matthew 1 - 2; Luke 1-2; John 1:1-18; Romans 8:3; Philippians 2:6-11; Colossians 1:13-22; Hebrews 1 - 2; 4:14 - 5:10; 1 John 1 - 2:2.

JESUS CHRIST *Son of God – his own claims:* Matthew 26:59-64; 27:41-44; Mark 2:1-12; John 5:17-47; 6:25-51; 7:16-31; 8:54-59; 10:22-39; 14:8-11; 17:1-5, 20-24; 19:7. Also God's word: Matthew 17:1-8; Mark 1:9-11.
– the opinion of his disciples and others: Matthew 16:13-20; 27:50-54; Mark 1:21-27; 5:1-13. Luke 1:31-35; John 1:29-34, 43-51; 6:66-69; 11:23-27; 20:28; Acts 2:22-36; 7:54-60; 9:17-22; 10:34-43; Romans 1:1-4; Ephesians 1:20-23; Philippians 2:5-11; Colossians 1:15-20; Hebrews 1; 1 John 1:1-4; 2:22-25; 4:9-10.
– for the evidence of his actions, see Miracles of Jesus.
Son of man: a real human being (yet sinless – Luke 4:1-13; 23:39-41; John 8:46; 2 Corinthians 5:21; Hebrews 4:15; 1 Peter 2:22-23; 3:18): Galatians 4:4; Matthew 4:2; 21:18; Mark 1:41; 10:21; Luke 7:13; John 4:6; 11:33, 35, 38; 13:1; 15:13; Acts 2:22-23; Hebrews 2:14-18; 4:15; 1 John 4:2.
The significance of his death: Mark 8:31-33; Luke 24:13-27, 44-48; John 1:29; 3:14-15; 11:50-52; 12:24; Acts 2:22-42; 3:12-26; 10:34-43; Romans 5:6-21; 1 Corinthians 11:23-26; Philippians 2:5-11; Hebrews 10:5-14; 1 Peter 2:24. See also under Forgiveness and Redemption.
The promise of his return: Matthew 24; 26:64; John 14; Acts 1:11; 3:19-21; Philippians 3:20; Colossians 3:4; 1 Thessalonians 1:10; 4:13-5:11; 2 Thessalonians 1:5 - 2:12; 2 Peter 3:8-13. See also Messiah.

JOY Psalms 16:11; 30:5; 43:4; 51:12; 126:5-6; Ecclesiastes 2:26; Isaiah 61:7; Jeremiah 15:16; Luke 15:7; John 15:11; 16:22; Romans 14:17; 15:13; Galatians 5:22; Philippians 1:4; 1 Thessalonians 2:20; 3:9; Hebrews 12:2; James 1:2; 1 Peter 1:8; Jude 24.

JUDGEMENT See Future destiny
JUSTIFICATION A legal term: acquittal. The New Testament declares that God can acquit man of breaking his law because the penalty has been paid in the death of Jesus (see also Forgiveness): Exodus 23:7; Job 13:18; 25:4; Psalms 51:1ff.; 103:6; 143:2; Isaiah 50:8-9; 53:11; Luke 18:14; Acts 13:39. Romans 2:13; 3:4, 19-30; 4:2ff.; 5:1-10; 8:30-34; 1 Corinthians 6:11; Galatians 2:15-21; 3:6-14; Titus 3:7; James 2:14-26.

KINGDOM God's rule: the new age (see special article 'The Kingdom of God and the Kingdom of Heaven', pp.484-485): Psalms 103:19; 145:11-13; Daniel 2:44; 4:3; 7:13-14, 27; Matthew 3:2; 4:23; 5:3, 10, 19-20; 6:9-10; 33; 13:11, 19, 24-52; 16:19, 28; 18:1-4, 23ff.; 19:12, 14, 23ff.; 20:1ff., 21ff; 21:43; 22:2ff.; 23:13; 24:14; 25:1ff., 34; 26:29; many similar references in Mark and Luke; John 3:3, 5; 18:36; Acts 14:22; 28:31; Romans 14:17; 1 Corinthians 4:20; Galatians 5:19-21; Colossians 1:13.

LAW God's instructions for right living.
Ritual and ceremonial law: Exodus 25 - 30; 34 - 40; Leviticus 1 - 9; 11 - 17; 22 - 25; Deuteronomy 14; 16; 18; 26.
Moral and social law: Exodus 20:1-17; 21 - 23; Leviticus 18 - 20; Deuteronomy 5:21; 10:12-21; 15; 19 - 25.
Delight in the law: Psalms 1; 19; 37:31; 40:8; 119; Proverbs 29:18.
Its permanent value: Matthew 5:17-20; 22:36-40; 23:23; Luke 10:25-28; Romans 3:31; 8:3-4.
The impossibility of meeting God's standards by human effort: the law's limitations: John 7:19; Acts 13:39; Romans 2:25-29; 3:19-21; 7:7-25; 8:3; Galatians 2:16; 3:21-24; Hebrews 7:18-19; James 2:8-12.

LIFE *Human life (creation)* Genesis 2:7, 9; Matthew 6:25, etc. etc.
God, the source of life; his life-giving laws and wisdom: Deuteronomy 30:15-20; Psalms 36:9; 133:3; Proverbs 8:35; 14:27; Jeremiah 21:8.
'Eternal' life (new creation): Matthew 7:14; 10:39; 16:25-26; 18:8-9, 19:16ff., 29; Luke 12:15; John 1:4; 3:15-16, 36, 4:14; 5:24; 6:27, 35, 40, 47-51; 10:10, 28; 11:25; 14:6; 17:3; 20:31. Romans 6:4ff., 22-23; 8:6; 2 Corinthians 4:10-12; 5:17ff.; Galatians 6:8; Ephesians 2:2ff.; 1 Timothy 6:12; 1 John 1:1-2; 3:14; 5:11-12; Revelation 22:1-2, 17.

LOVE 1 Corinthians 13; Galatians 5:22; 1 John 4:7 - 5:3.
The love of God. Christ's love: Deuteronomy 7:7-8; Proverbs 3:12; Isaiah 63:7-9; Jeremiah 31:3; Hosea 3:1; 14:4; John 3:16; 13:1; 15:9, 12-13; Romans 8:35-39; Galatians 2:20; Ephesians 2:4; 3:17-19; Hebrews 12:6; 1 John 3:1.
Man's love for God: Exodus 20:6; Deuteronomy 6:5; 11:1, 13, 22; Psalms 31:23; 116:1; 119:47-48; John 14:15, 21-24; Romans 8:28; 1 Corinthians 8:3; 1 Peter 1:8.
Loving others: Leviticus 19:18, 34; Matthew 5:43-46; John 13:34-35; 14:15, 21-24; 15:9-14; Galatians 5:13-14; Ephesians 4:2, 15-16; Philippians 2:2; Hebrews 10:24; 1 John 4:7 - 5:3.
Love between man and woman: Genesis 29:20; 2 Samuel 13:15; Proverbs 5:18-19;

Song of Solomon; Ephesians 5:25ff.; Colossians 3:19.

MAN Created by God – with a mortal, yet moral and spiritual nature – to worship, obey and enjoy his friendship: Genesis 1 - 2; 17:1ff., etc.; Deuteronomy 5:28-33; 8; 2 Samuel 19:12-13; Psalms 8; 27; 66; 78:5-8; Isaiah 40:6-8; 43; Ecclesiastes 12:1-7; Micah 6:6-8; Luke 12:13-21; Romans 1:18-25; 8:18ff.; 1 Corinthians 15:45-50; 2 Corinthians 5:1-5; 6:16-18.
In rebellion against God: Genesis 3; Judges 2:11-23; Psalm 2:1-3; Daniel 9:3-19; Romans 1 - 3; 7:13-25. Hebrews 3:7-19; Revelation 17 - 18. See also Sin and evil.
For man's re-creation in Christ and glorious destiny, see Future destiny, Life Regeneration, Heaven, etc.

MEDIATOR The go-between, reconciling God and man (see also Reconciliation): Galatians 3:19-20; 1 Timothy 2:5; Hebrews 8:6; 9:15; 12:24.

MERCY Kindness; readiness to forgive (see also Grace): Exodus 34:6-7; Nehemiah 9:7, 31; Psalms 23:6; 25:6; 40:11; 51:1; 103:4, 8; Daniel 9:9; Jonah 4:2; Micah 6:8; Matthew 5:7; Luke 18:13; Romans 9:15; 12:1; Ephesians 2:4.

MESSIAH The Christ – God's chosen deliverer: Deuteronomy 18:15ff.; Psalms 2; 45:6-7; 72; 110; Isaiah 9:2-7; 11; 42:1-9; 49:1-6; 52:13 - 53:12; 61:1-3; Jeremiah 23:5-6; 33:14-16; Ezekiel 34:22ff.; Daniel 7; Zechariah 9:9-10; Matthew 1:18, 22-23; 16:16, 20; 26:63; Mark 14:61-62; Luke 2:11, 26; John 4:25, 29; 7:26-27, 31, 41-42; 9:22; Acts 2:36; 3:20-21; 4:26-28; 18:28; 26:22-23.

PEACE Numbers 6:26; Psalms 4:8; 85:8-10; 119:165; Proverbs 3:17; Isaiah 9:6-7; 57:19-21; Jeremiah 6:14; 16:5; Ezekiel 34:25; Matthew 10:34; Luke 1:79; 2:14; 7:50; 19:38, 42; John 14:27; Acts 10:36; Romans 1:7; 5:1; 8:6; 14:19; Galatians 5:22; Ephesians 2:14-17; 4:3; 6:15; Philippians 4:7; Colossians 3:15; 2 Thessalonians 3:16; James 3:17-18.

PRAYER See Prayers of the Bible. Jesus' teaching on prayer: Matthew 6:5-15; 7:7-11; 26:41; Mark 12:38-40; 13:33; 14:38; Luke 11:1-13; 18:1-14.

RECONCILIATION *Between God and man:* Romans 5:6-11; 11:15; 2 Corinthians 5:18-20; Colossians 1:20-22.
Between men: Matthew 5:23-24; John 17:11, 20-23; 1 Corinthians 7:11; 12:12ff.; Galatians 3:28; Ephesians 2:11-22.

REDEMPTION Payment of a price to buy deliverance and freedom: Leviticus 25:25-55; Exodus 13:13; 21:30; 30:12; Numbers 18:15-16.
God's redemption of his people: Exodus 6:6; Deuteronomy 7:8; 21:8; 2 Samuel 4:9; Job 33:22-28; Psalms 103:4; 107:2; 130:8; Isaiah 50:2; 63:9; Hosea 13:14.
Christ as a ransom: Matthew 20:28; Romans 3:24; 8:23; 1 Corinthians 1:30; Galatians 3:13; Ephesians 1:7; 4:30; Colossians 1:14; Hebrews 9:12, 15; 1 Peter 1:18-19; Revelation 5:9; 14:3, 4.

REGENERATION Being re-born, re-created, made alive to God: Psalm 51:10; Jeremiah 24:7; 31:33-34; Ezekiel 11:19; 36:26; Matthew 19:28; John 1:12-13; 3:3ff.;

Romans 8:9ff.; 2 Corinthians 5:17;
Ephesians 2:5; Titus 3:5; 1 Peter 1:23;
1 John 2:29; 3:9; 4:7; 5:1, 4, 18.

REPENTANCE Turning from sin and self-
centredness to God: 2 Kings 17:13; 23:25;
2 Chronicles 33:10ff.; Job 42:6; Psalms 51;
78:34; Isaiah 1:16-20; 55:6ff.; Jeremiah
3:12-14; Ezekiel 33:12ff.; Daniel 9:3-20;
Hosea 14:1ff.; Joel 2:12-14; Matthew 3:2, 8;
11:20-21; Mark 1:4; Luke 5:32; 13:3, 5; 15:7,
10, 18-21; 24:47; Acts 2:38; 17:30; 20:21;
26:20; 2 Corinthians 7:10; Hebrews 12:17;
2 Peter 3:9; Revelation 2:5.

RESURRECTION Being raised from death
to a new life (a bodily resurrection like
Christ's): Job 19:25-27; Psalm 49:14-15;
Isaiah 26:19; Ezekiel 37; Daniel 12:2;
Matthew 22:30-32; Luke 14:14; 20:34-38;
John 5:29; 6:39-40, 44, 54; 11:25; Acts
2:22-36; 4:33; 17:18, 32; 23:6-8; 24:15;
Romans 1:4; 4:24-25; 6:5ff.; 1 Corinthians
15; Philippians 3:10-11; Colossians 2:12;
3:1-4; 1 Thessalonians 4:13ff.; Hebrews
11:35; 1 Peter 1:3; 3:21; 1 John 3:2; Revelation 20:4-6, 11-15.
Accounts of Jesus' resurrection: Matthew
28; Mark 16; Luke 24; John 20; 1 Corinthians 15:3-8.

REVELATION What God makes known to
man. The whole Bible is God's revelation;
these references simply pinpoint some
examples: Deuteronomy 29:29; 1 Samuel
3:7, 21; Isaiah 22:14; 40:5; Daniel 2:22,
28ff.; Amos 3:7; Luke 17:30; John 12:38;
Romans 1:17-18; 2:5; 8:18; 16:25; 1 Corinthians 14:6, 26; 2 Corinthians 12:1, 7; Galatians 1:12; 3:23; Ephesians 1:9-10, 17; 3:3,
5; 1 Peter 1:5, 12-13; 5:1; Revelation 1:1.
Christ as the revelation of God: e.g. John
1:1-18; 14:7; Colossians 1:15ff.; Hebrews
1:1-3; 2 Peter 1:16ff.; 1 John 1:1ff.; Revelation 1:12-16.
God revealed in his creation: Job 38 - 40;
Psalms 8; 19; 104; Romans 1.
*God specially revealed in his power and
glory:* Exodus 24:9-11; 33:18 - 34:9; 1 Kings
19:9ff.; Isaiah 6; Ezekiel 1; 10; Daniel
7:9-14; Matthew 17:1-5 (Christ's transfiguration); Revelation 4.

RIGHTEOUSNESS The right action and
justice which characterize God and which
he requires of men. Genesis 15:6; 18:23ff.;
Leviticus 19:15; Deuteronomy 4:8; Job 4:7;
36:7; Psalms 1:5-6; 11:7; 23:3; 34:19; 37:25;
97:6; 98:9; Proverbs 10:2; 11:4ff.; Isaiah
53:11; 64:6; Ezekiel 3:20-21; 33:12ff.;

Habakkuk 1:4, 13; Matthew 5:6, 10, 20;
6:33; 9:13; 13:43; Luke 18:9; John 16:8-10;
Romans 3:10-26; 4:3ff.; 5:17ff.; 6:13ff.;
10:3ff.; 2 Corinthians 5:21; 6:14; Ephesians
6:14; Philippians 1:11; Hebrews 12:11;
James 5:16; 1 Peter 2:24; 2 Peter 3:13;
1 John 2:1; 3:7.

SACRIFICE *Old Testament sacrifice and
offerings:* Genesis 4:2-4; 8:20; 22:1-14;
Exodus 12 (the Passover); 29 - 30; Leviticus 1 - 9; 16 (the Atonement); 17; 1 Samuel
15:22; Psalms 50:5; 51:15-19; 107:22;
Proverbs 15:8; Isaiah 43:23-24; Jeremiah
6:20; Hosea 3:4; Amos 4:4-5; 5:21-24.
In the New Testament: Matthew 9:13; 26:28;
Luke 2:24; John 1:29; 6:51ff.; Romans 12:1;
1 Corinthians 10:14ff.; Ephesians 5:2;
Philippians 2:17; 4:18; Hebrews 5:1-3; 7:27;
9:11-28; 10; 13:15-16; 1 Peter 2:5.

SALVATION God's rescue of man from sin
and death to 'eternal' life, a new quality
and dimension of existence. The theme of
salvation—God as saviour—runs right
through the Bible. It is the heart of the
Christian message: Exodus 14:30; Numbers
10:9; Deuteronomy 33:29; Judges 2:16-18;
1 Samuel 15:23; 1 Chronicles 11:14; Job
22:29; Psalms 28:8-9; 34:6; 37:40; Isaiah
30:15; 43:11-13; 45:21-22; 59:1; Jeremiah
30:10-11; Hosea 13:4; Matthew 1:21; 10:22;
19:25; 27:42; Luke 2:11; 8:12; John 3:17;
10:9; Acts 2:21; 4:12; 16:30-31; Romans
5:9-10; 10:9-13; 1 Corinthians 3:15; Ephesians 2:8; 1 Timothy 1:15; 2:4; 4:10;
Hebrews 7:25. Salvation is also described
in a series of metaphors or pictures: God
covers man's sin—see Atonement; he
acquits—see Justification; he reconciles
—see Reconciliation; he redeems—see
Redemption; he gives new life—see Regeneration and Life. See also Gospel.

SANCTIFICATION Making holy, setting
apart for God (see Holiness); having an in-
creasingly Christ-like character: Exodus
31:12-15; Leviticus 22:9; Deuteronomy 5:12;
Joshua 3:5; 1 Chronicles 15:14; Ezekiel
37:24-28; John 10:36; 15:1-17; 17:17-19;
Romans 12:1ff.; 15:16; 1 Corinthians 1:2,
30; 6:11; 7:14; Ephesians 4:24; Philippians
1:9-11, 27; Colossians 1:10; 1 Thessalonians 3:11-13; 4:3-4; 5:23; 2 Thessalonians 2:13; 1 Timothy 4:5; Hebrews 10:10,
14, 29, 2 Peter 1:3-11; 1 John 3:2-3.

SIN AND EVIL Wrong-doing; disobedience;
rebellion against God. *Its coming into the
world:* Genesis 2 - 3; 2 Peter 2:4; Jude 5-7;

Revelation 12:7-12.
*Satan—the personification of evil—and his
work:* Genesis 3:1-6; Job 1 - 2; Matthew
4:1-11; 12:22-28; 16:23; Luke 13:16; 22:3-6,
31; John 8:43-47; Acts 26:15-18; 2 Corinthians 2:10-11; 11:14; 12:7; 1 Thessalonians
2:18; Hebrews 2:14; 1 Peter 5:8; 1 John
3:8-10; Revelation 2:13; 12:7-17.
*The universality of sin, and its effect on
man:* Genesis 3:16-24; 4; Deuteronomy
9:6-24; Psalm 14; Isaiah 59:1ff.; Jeremiah
44; Ezekiel 36:22-32; Matthew 15:16-20;
Romans 1:28-32; 5:12; 6:23; Galatians
5:19-21; Ephesians 2:1-3; James 1:12-15;
4:1-3, 17; 1 John 3:4.
God's victory; sin's ultimate destruction:
Psalm 103; Romans 5:15-21; 1 Corinthians
15:54-57; 1 John 3:4-10; Revelation 20.

SPIRIT Mind, heart, will; spirit as distinct
from, or opposed to 'flesh' (see above; see
also Holy Spirit): 2 Kings 2:9; Job 32:18;
Psalms 31:5; 34:18; 51:10; Isaiah 26:9;
31:3; Ezekiel 37:1-10 ('breath' and 'spirit'
translate the same Hebrew word); Matthew
5:3; 26:41; John 3:6; 4:23-24; Romans
2:29; 8; 1 Corinthians 2:11ff.; Galatians
5:16-25; Ephesians 4:23.

TEMPTATION Trial, testing: Genesis 3;
22:1; Exodus 17:7; Deuteronomy 6:16;
Psalm 95:9; Matthew 6:13; 22:35; 26:41;
Acts 5:9; 1 Corinthians 7:5; 10:9-13;
Hebrews 2:18; 4:15; James 1:2-4, 13-15.
The temptation of Jesus: Matthew 4:1-11;
Mark 1:12-13; Luke 4:1-13.

WISDOM The expression of an attitude to
life which is centred on God and his laws:
Exodus 28:3; Deuteronomy 34:9; 1 Kings
3:5-14; Job 12:13; 28; Psalms 37:30; 104:24;
Proverbs 1; 8; 9; Ecclesiastes 1:13-18;
2:12-26; Isaiah 11:2; Daniel 2:20-23; Matthew 13:54; Luke 2:52; 21:15; Acts 6:3;
1 Corinthians 1:17 - 2:16; 3:18ff.; Colossians 3:16; 2 Timothy 3:15; James 1:5;
3:13-18.

WORLD *The created universe; the earth:*
2 Samuel 22:16; Job 34:13; Psalms 24:1;
50:12; 90:2; Matthew 4:8; 16:26; John 1:9;
Romans 5:12.
Mankind: Psalm 9:8; Isaiah 13:11; Luke
2:1; John 3:16-17; 8:26; 14:31; 1 Corinthians 1:21.
The present age: Matthew 24:3; 28:20; Luke
18:30; Ephesians 1:21.
The world in rebellion against God: John
7:7; 8:23; 14:17; 15:18-19; James 4:4;
1 John 2:15-17; 4:4-5; 5:4-5.